BETTER
CHURCH BULLETINS

BETTER CHURCH BULLETINS

Including
Hints and Helps for the Bulletin Board

Stella O. Barnett

Fleming H. Revell Company

Printed in the United States of America

LIBRARY OF CONGRESS CATALOG CARD NUMBER: 55–6631

Westwood, N.J.—316 Third Avenue
Los Angeles 41—2173 Colorado Boulevard
London E.C. 4—29 Ludgate Hill
Glasgow C. 2—229 Bothwell Street

CONTENTS

5

INTRODUCTION

THE CHURCH BULLETIN is the silent partner in your ministry. Through an appropriate front page message, you can create a spirit of reverence preparatory to the sermon. A well-planned bulletin impresses and instructs; it is a visual part of your worship service to be carried into the home and passed on to others, who may be inspired by the Word of God.

This book has been compiled for the busy pastor, educational director and church secretary. It includes poems and quotations, interspersed with "inspirettes," which will prove helpful in the preparation of church bulletins, sermons and youth programs.

Editors of church, club, school and fraternity periodicals will find alphabetized, inspirational poems, quick quotes, and anecdotes at their finger tips.

BETTER
CHURCH BULLETINS

I

ORDER OF SERVICES

PREREQUISITE TO AN effective, inspiring, and reverent service is a well-planned and smoothly-coordinated order of worship. The following services are offered merely as examples, and need not be followed with any degree of exactness; they are offered in the hope that they may present a few new or fresh ideas for the church service.

MORNING

ORGAN PRELUDE
STRIKING THE HOUR
DOXOLOGY
INVOCATION
GLORIA
    (Ushers will seat those waiting)
HYMN
SCRIPTURE READING
HYMN MEDITATION
MORNING PRAYER

15

RESPONSE

(Ushers will seat those waiting)

*HYMN

OFFERTORY PRAYER

OFFERTORY HYMN

SERMON

*HYMN

BENEDICTION AND CHORAL RESPONSE

EVENING

PRELUDE

*HYMN

PRAYER

HYMN

SCRIPTURE READING

HYMN

OFFERTORY PRAYER

OFFERTORY HYMN

SERMON

*HYMN

BENEDICTION

MORNING WORSHIP

Our Morning Worship starts with the first note of the organ—therefore, let us be Worshipers from that moment!

ORGAN MEDITATION

CHORAL CALL TO WORSHIP

* Indicates when the congregation stands

PROCESSIONAL HYMN

PRAYER OF INVOCATION

CAROL CHOIR

THE RESPONSIVE READING

SOLO

THE PASTORAL PRAYER

WORSHIP THROUGH TITHES AND OFFERINGS

OFFERTORY

HYMN OF DEDICATION

PRAYER OF DEDICATION

THE SCRIPTURE READING

CHOIR RECESSIONAL

SERMON

HYMN OF INVITATION

BENEDICTION AND CHORAL RESPONSE

POSTLUDE

Morning Worship

Let the first tone of the organ be a call to reverent silence in which all may become aware of His presence.

ORGAN PRELUDE

DOXOLOGY, INVOCATION GLORIA PATRI

HYMN

WELCOME AND ANNOUNCEMENTS

ANTHEM

SCRIPTURE READING

MORNING PRAYER

HYMN

OFFERTORY

SERMON

INVITATION HYMN

BENEDICTION AND CHORAL RESPONSE

Enter to Worship—Depart to Serve

EVENING WORSHIP

ORGAN PRELUDE

HYMN

HYMN

SCRIPTURAL READING

EVENING PRAYER

HYMN

HYMN

OFFERTORY

SPECIAL MUSIC

SERMON

INVITATION

BENEDICTION

POSTLUDE

MORNING WORSHIP

PRELUDE

DOXOLOGY

INVOCATION—THE LORD'S PRAYER

HYMN

SCRIPTURE READING

PRAYER—RESPONSE

HYMN
OFFERTORY
ANTHEM
SERMON
HYMN
BENEDICTION
POSTLUDE

Evening Worship

PRELUDE
HYMN
SCRIPTURE READING
PRAYER
HYMN
OFFERTORY
SOLO
SERMON
HYMN
BENEDICTION
POSTLUDE

Morning Worship

The Lord is in His Holy Temple: let all the earth keep silence before Him.

ORGAN PRELUDE
THE DOXOLOGY
INVOCATION
GLORIA PATRI

READING OF SCRIPTURE

> *Ushers requested to seat no one during reading of Scripture or Special Music*

ORGAN RESPONSE

PRAYER

ANNOUNCEMENTS

HYMN

OFFERTORY PRAYER

OFFERTORY

SERMON

HYMN

BENEDICTION

ORGAN POSTLUDE

Evening Worship

> *The Lord is in His Holy Temple: let all the earth keep silence before Him.*

ORGAN PRELUDE

HYMN

READING OF SCRIPTURE

> *Ushers requested to seat no one during reading of Scripture or Special Music*

ORGAN RESPONSE

PRAYER

ANNOUNCEMENTS

HYMN

OFFERTORY PRAYER

OFFERTORY

SERMON

HYMN
BENEDICTION
ORGAN POSTLUDE

The Morning Hour of Worship

THE ORGAN PRELUDE
CHIMES IN THE CALL TO WORSHIP
DOXOLOGY, CONGREGATION STANDING
THE INVOCATION
GLORIA PATRI
WORSHIP THROUGH THE BRINGING OF TITHES AND OFFER-
    INGS
ORGAN OFFERTORY
HYMN OF PREPARATION
READING OF THE SCRIPTURE AND RESPONSE
THE MORNING PRAYER
SOLO
SERMON
HYMN OF INVITATION
BENEDICTION
THE ORGAN POSTLUDE

The Evening Hour of Worship

ORGAN AND PIANO PRELUDE
HYMN OF THE EVENING
READING OF THE SCRIPTURE
RECEIVING OF THE OFFERING
THE EVENING PRAYER—ORGAN AND PIANO OFFERTORY
HYMN
RESPONSIVE READING

SOLO

SERMON

HYMN OF INVITATION

BENEDICTION

ORGAN AND PIANO POSTLUDE

II

BULLETIN BOARD SENTENCES

JANUARY

First week—For religion, the good is indeed real, for in the end nothing else is real.
—Bernard Bosanquet

Second week—Faith has nothing to fear from thinking.—Albert Schweitzer

Third week—There is a moral as well as a military strategy.—R. H. Tweney

Fourth week—In all churches individuals are better than their creeds.—William E. Channing

Fifth week—Every man is entitled to be valued by his best moment.—Ralph Waldo Emerson

FEBRUARY

First week—Lincoln's birthday
The dogmas of the past are inadequate to the stormy present.—Abraham Lincoln

Second week—Brotherhood week
Hate the evil, and love the good, and establish judgment in the gate.—Amos 5:15

Third week—Washington's birthday
> The liberty you possess is the work of common dangers, sufferings, and successes.—George Washington

Fourth week—Trouble is the necessary salt of life without which life loses its savor.—Arnold J. Toynbee

MARCH

First week—This country is entrusted by God with a mission for humanity.—William E. Channing

Second week—Beauty is a sacrament conferring grace beyond merit.—Harold Scott

Third week—The subject matter of statecraft is the Soul of Man.—Judge Learned Hand

Fourth week—Thou shalt love the Lord thy God with all thy heart and with all thy soul.—Mark 12:30

APRIL

First week—Reason, conscience, by which we discover the true and the right are immortal as their Author.—W. E. Channing

Second week—Plough deep while sluggards sleep.
> —Benjamin Franklin

Third week—America's independence will implant liberty and make it flourish throughout the world.—Marquis de Lafayette

Fourth week—Art and Science have been martyrs equally with Religion.—William Temple

MAY

First week—God humanizes himself and enters into social relations with us.—Leibnitz

Second week—Words are wise men's counters, but they are the money of fools.—Thomas Hobbes

Third week—Let justice roll down as waters, and righteousness as an overflowing stream.—Amos 5:24

Fourth week—Trust thyself; every heart vibrates to that iron string.—Emerson

Fifth week—Memorial Day

In the remembrance of a glorious past individuals and nations find their noblest inspiration.—Sir William Temple

JUNE

First week—Gold is no bulwark to the arrogant who spurn the great altar of God's justice.—Aeschylus

Second week—The supreme task of our generation is to give a soul to world-consciousness.—S. Radhakrishnan

Third week—He who denies his basic equality with another is anti-democratic.—Paul Weiss

Fourth week—With what measure ye mete, it shall be measured to you again.—Matthew 7:12

JULY

First week—Independence Day

The core of our defense is the faith we have in the institutions we defend.—Franklin D. Roosevelt

Second week—I am determined that no man shall drag me down by making me hate him.—Booker T. Washington

Third week—So do your work in the world that others may do their work better.—Felix Adler

Fourth week—Unto whomsoever much is given, of him shall much be required.—Luke 12:48

AUGUST

First week—A good example is like a bell that calls many to church.—Danish proverb

Second week—In much wisdom is much grief: and he that increaseth knowledge increaseth sorrow.—Ecclesiastes 12:12

Third week—Where love is, there is God.—Tolstoy

Fourth week—Thou shalt not follow a multitude to do evil.—Exodus 23:2

Fifth week—Labor Day
In America we insist that the employer-employee relationship be one between free men and equals.—Franklin D. Roosevelt

SEPTEMBER

First week—Be ashamed to die before you have won some victory for humanity.—Horace Mann

Second week—Minds are like parachutes—they only function when open.—Thomas Dewar

Third week—Above all things have fervent charity among yourselves; for charity covers a multitude of sins.—Peter 4:8

Fourth week—A ship ought not to be held by one anchor, nor life by a single hope.—Epictetus

OCTOBER

First week—We must make our decisions in the conviction that all men are created equal.—Harry S. Truman

Second week—None are so likely to believe too little as those who have begun with believing too much.—W. E. Channing

Third week—I shall adopt new views as far as they appear to be true views.—Abraham Lincoln

Fourth week—United Nations' Day
Freedom is something so priceless that no sacrifice is too great to preserve it.—Morris Cohen

NOVEMBER

First week—The end of government is the good of the community.—John Locke

Second week—In heroism life's supreme mystery is hidden.—William James.

Third week—None of us liveth to himself and no man dieth to himself.—Romans 11:7

Fourth week—Thanksgiving Day
The Lord will rejoice over thee for good, as he rejoiced over thy fathers.—Deuteronomy 30:9

Fifth week—There is nothing so sacred as the human soul.—John Haynes Holmes

DECEMBER

First week—Find joy in the Eternal; set not your heart on another's possessions.—Upanishads

Second week—Be ye therefore merciful, as your Father also is merciful.—Luke 6:36

Third week—Christmas Day

Glory to God in the highest, and on earth peace, good will toward men.—Luke 2:14

Fourth week—New Year's Day

It is the molding and the greatness of souls that we really care for.—Bernard Bosanquet

Extra Bulletin Board Sentences

January, February and March

May I wish no victory that harms either me or my opponent.—Eusebius

Every lofty religious mind belongs not to the church but to religious humanity.—Albert Schweitzer

The destiny of mankind hangs in the balance of what we say and what we accomplish.—Dwight D. Eisenhower

Nothing in life has value except to do right and fear not.—Gilbert Murray

A brother offended is harder to be won than a strong city.—Proverbs 18:19

With malice toward none; with charity for all; let us strive on to finish the work we are in.—Abraham Lincoln

Observe good faith and justice towards all nations.—George Washington

Inasmuch as ye have done it unto one of the least of these my brethren, ye have done it unto me.—Matthew 25:40

All that is necessary for the triumph of evil is that good men do nothing.—Edmund Burke

The love of God blooms in the lilac, murmers in the brook, shines in the dawn, sings in the bird. The love of God is the truest key of knowledge.—Anonymous

If thou thinkest twice before thou speakest once, Thou wilt speak twice the better for it.—Wm. Penn

Let us be silent that we may hear the whisper of God.—Emerson

In giving freedom to the slave we assure freedom to the free—honorable alike in what we give and what we preserve.—Abraham Lincoln

APRIL, MAY AND JUNE

He that loveth not knoweth not God; for God is love. I John 4:8

Palm Sunday—All great prayer is born out of intense earnestness.—Rufus M. Jones

Easter—Spend your life so that you deserve to be immortal.—Unamuno

Zeal is very blind when it encroaches upon the rights of others.—P. Quesnel

Every man's highest, nameless though it be, is his living God.—James Martineau

God incarnates himself in man and evermore goeth forth anew to take possession of his World.—Ralph Waldo Emerson

Life is not a vessel to be drained, but a cup to be filled.—Chinese proverb

It is better to guard speech than to guard wealth.—
Lucian

Atheism is rather in the life than in the heart of a man.
—Francis Bacon

I have always thought that faith in immortality is
proof of the sanity of a man's nature.—Emerson

God will keep no nation in supreme peace that will
not do supreme duty.—William McKinley

Promise yourself to be so strong that nothing can dis-
turb your peace of mind.—Anonymous

JULY, AUGUST AND SEPTEMBER

Labor to cast self aside, and to live in the universal life.
—Josiah Royce

We cannot do evil to others without doing it to ourselves.—Desmahis

We have climbed out of the dark only because a few
dared to walk ahead and face the sun.—Anna
Garlin Spencer

Goodness is the only investment that never fails.—
Thoreau

When he giveth quietness, who then can make trouble?—Job 34:29

The sanctity of the inner life is fundamental in Jesus'
teaching.—William W. Fenn

The soul is dyed the color of the leisure hours.—Anonymous

The youth of a nation are the trustees of posterity.—
Benjamin Disraeli.

Jesus in His person reveals man in full measure, at
once man and hero.—H. B. Alexander

Most conversions are made to sects, few to truth and love.—Lucretia Mott

OCTOBER, NOVEMBER AND DECEMBER

There is a statement of religion possible which makes all skepticism absurd.—Emerson

Democracy and freedom are eternal laws of the human spirit.—Dwight D. Eisenhower

Great peace have they which love thy law.—Psalm 119:165

All experience is an arch to build upon.—Henry Brooks Adams

I do not know any religion apart from human activity. —Gandhi

The story of the evolution of life on this globe is the most enthralling in science.—Jan Christian Smuts

Let man learn the revelation of all nature and all thought to his heart.—Ralph Waldo Emerson

Religion is goodness with its sleeves rolled up.—Magnus Ratter

The aim of religion is not to get us into heaven, but to get heaven into us.—Ulysses G. B. Pierce

We have committed the Golden Rule to memory; let us now commit it to life.—Edwin Markham.

To find his place and fill it is success for a man.—Phillips Brooks.

III

QUICK QUOTES FOR BULLETIN
AND BULLETIN BOARD

THE PRIVILEGE OF prayer to me is one of my most cherished possessions, because faith and experience alike convince me that God Himself sees and answers, and His answers I never venture to criticize. It is only my part to ask. It is entirely His to give or withhold as He knows is best. In the quiet of the home, in the heat of life and strife, in the face of death, the privilege of speech with God is inestimable. I value it more because it calls for nothing that the wayfaring man, though a fool, cannot give—that is, the simplest expression of his simplest desire.

—Sir Wilfred Grenfell

If the outlook is dark, try the uplook.

—Baptist Observer

Perhaps the funmaker, who said, "Speak well of your enemies—remember you made them," had it about right. At least most of the differences in life result from our getting offended, not the other fellow.

—The Messenger

When a man becomes a true Christian, he becomes industrious, trustworthy, and prosperous.

—John Wesley

If you would be happy be active as a running stream, not cloudy and morbid as a stagnant pool.

—The Watchword

Experience is not what happens to a man. It is what a man does with what happens to him.

—Aldous Huxley

Garments of righteousness never go out of style.

—Western Recorder

Heaven is a prepared place for a prepared people.

—Moody

It is better to live rich than to die rich.

—Watchword

No man ever prayed without learning something.

—Emerson

The Divine Scriptures are the feast of wisdom, and the single books are the various dishes.

—Ambrose

The men whom I have seen succeed best in life have always been cheerful and hopeful men who went about their business with a smile on their faces and took the changes and chances of this mortal life like men, facing rough and smooth alike as it came.

—Charles Kingsley

8/21/55

True obedience to God is faith and good works. He is truly obedient who trusts Him and does what He commands.

—Martin Luther

I believe in the supreme worth of the individual and in his right to life, liberty and the pursuit of happiness.

—Edwin Markham

Real "quality folk" are rich, but their wealth is the affluence of character.

—Christian Union Herald

When a man lives with God, his voice shall be as sweet as the murmur of the brook and the rustle of the corn.

—Emerson

Character is not made in a crisis—it is only exhibited.

—Dr. Robert Freeman

A child of God should be a visible beatitude for joy and happiness, and a living doxology for gratitude and adoration.

—Spurgeon

The man who has begun to live more seriously within, begins to live more simply without.

—Phillips Brooks

Quiet minds cannot be perplexed or frightened, but go on in fortune or misfortune at their own private pace, like a clock during a thunderstorm.

—Stevenson

Faith in God gives the ability to find God's plans.

—Rev. W. R. Newhall

By their missionary giving shall ye know them.

—Christian Advocate

Books are the quietest and most constant of friends: they are the most accessible and wisest of counselors, and the most patient of teachers.

—Charles W. Eliot

How easy it is to forget that the things of the spirit are so much more powerful than material things.

—Selected

"God give me the serenity to accept what cannot be changed; give me courage to change what can be changed, and the wisdom to know one from the other."

—Reinhold Niebuhr

Cheerfulness and contentment are great beautifiers and are famous preservers of youthful looks.

—Anonymous

"If there are two rugs in your room, one before the mirror and before the bed, which one will be worn out first?"

—D. L. Moody

Make peace with what has happened, don't foolishly regret it. A blunder has no power, as soon as you forget it.

—Author Unknown

Do today's duty, fight today's temptation, and do not weaken and distract yourself by looking forward to things you cannot see, and could not understand if you saw them.

—Kingsley

No matter what the world thinks about religious experience, the one who possesses it has the treasure of a thing that has given to life meaning and beauty and a new splendor to the world and to mankind.

—Carl Gustav Jung

There is a very simple test by which, it is said, we can tell good people from bad. If a smile improves a man's face, he is a good man; if a smile disfigures his face, he is a bad man.

—William Lyon Phelps

Whatever may be the mysteries of life and death, there is one mystery which the cross of Christ reveals to us, and that is the infinite love and absolute goodness of God.

—Charles Kingsley

An egotist is not a man who thinks too much of himself; he is a man who thinks too little of other people!

—Joseph Fort Newton

It is not the fact that a man has riches which keeps him from the kingdom of heaven, but the fact that riches have him.

—Caird

Wisdom is knowing what to do next; skill is knowing how to do it, and virtue is doing it.

—David Starr Jordan

In the course of my observation, the disputing, contradicting and confuting people are generally unfortunate in their affairs. They get victory sometimes, but they never get goodwill, which would be of more use to them.

—Benjamin Franklin

———————

The best jobs haven't been started. The best work hasn't been done.

—Berton Braley

———————

Depression, gloom, pessimism, despair, discouragement, these slay ten human beings to every one murdered by typhoid, influenza, diabetes or pneumonia. If tuberculosis is the great white plague, fear is the great black plague. Be cheerful.

—Dr. Frank Crane

———————

I divide the world in three classes—the few who make things happen, the many who watch things happen, and the overwhelming majority who have no notion of what happens.

—Nicholas Murray Butler

———————

Did you ever hear of a man who had striven all his life faithfully and singly toward a thing and in no measure obtained it?

—Thoreau

———————

Humility is perfect quietness of heart. It is to have no trouble. It is never to be fretted or irritated or sore or disappointed. It is to expect nothing, to wonder at nothing that is done to me. It is to be at rest when nobody praises me and when I am blamed or despised. It is to have a blessed home in the Lord, where I can go in and shut the door and kneel to my Father in secret, and am at peace as in the deep sea of calmness when all around and above is trouble.

—Andrew Murray

———————

The longer we dwell on our misfortunes the greater is their power to harm us.

—Voltaire

6/19/55   ———————

Men are not made religious by performing certain actions which are externally good, but they must first have righteous principles, and then they will not fail to perform virtuous actions.

—Martin Luther

———————

It is something to make two blades of grass grow where only one was growing; it is much more to have been the occasion of the planting of an oak which shall defy twenty scores of winters, or of an elm which shall canopy with its green cloud of foliage half as many generations of mortal immortalities.

—Oliver Wendell Holmes

Justice without power is inefficient; power without justice is tyranny. . . . Justice and power must therefore be brought together so that whatever is just may be powerful and whatever is powerful may be just.

—Pascal

Reverence is one of the signs of strength; irreverence one of the surest indications of weakness. No man will rise high who jeers at sacred things. The fine loyalties of life must be reverenced or they will be foresworn in the day of trial.

—Anonymous

IV

POEMS AND INSPIRATIONAL PIECES

1. AGE

BLESSINGS OF EVENING

Abide with us: for it is toward evening, and the day is far spent. (Luke 24:29)

Some people have a special fondness for the early hours of the day. The brightening light, the dewdrop, and the morning-glory appeal to them. They are charmed with the freshness and the promise of the day that is to come; and so am I.

But somehow, of all the hours, the evening to me is the best. It may have been a day of storm and cloud, but the storm is over and the clouds have largely passed away, and the calm, quiet, happy time has come.

Evening reminds me of old age. It is the setting sun, deepening into the twilight of life. The day, too, may have its heat, its work, its noise, its cares and troubles, but these are over, and every cloud from North to South and from East to West is shot through and through with the golden glories of the sunset. "At evening time it shall be light."

Sweet memories cluster about the evening, and though the night is coming on, it makes the morning that much nearer, and all is well. The wise man has truly said, "The hoary head is a crown of glory, if it be found in the way of righteousness."

A. U. Boone

Let Me Grow Lovely

Let me grow lovely, growing old—
    So many fine things do;
Laces, and ivory, and gold,
    And silks need not be new;

And there is healing in old trees,
    Old streets a glamour hold;
Why may not I, as well as these,
    Grow lovely, growing old?

By permission of Karle Wilson Baker

If I Can Grow Old Like a Garden

If I can grow old like a garden,
I never shall mind growing old.
The summer will die, and the autumn
Weave garlands of scarlet and gold.

But beauty will burnish my garden
With glorious yellows and blues,

The sunrise will touch it with silver;
The sunset with lavender hues.

When winter winds blow on my garden,
The roses will all be asleep
And a blanket of snowflakes above them
The souls of the roses will keep.

If I can grow old like a garden,
My soul will awake in the spring,
For death will be only a winter
To prepare for new blossoming.

—Anne Campbell

HAND IN HAND

I have seen a line of snow-white birds
Drawn across an evening sky.
I have seen divine, unspoken words
Shining in a lover's eye.
I have seen moonlight on a mountaintop
Silver and cool and still.
I have heard church bells faintly echoing
Over a distant hill.
Close enough to beauty I have been,
And, in all the whole wide land,
Here's the sweetest sight that I have seen—
One old couple walking hand in hand.

—Author unknown

2. CHASTENING

CALAMITY—OFTEN BLESSING

The story is told of an only survivor of a shipwreck who was thrown upon an uninhabited island. After a while he managed to build for himself a rude hut in which he placed the "little all" that he had saved from the sinking ship. He prayed to God for deliverance, and anxiously scanned the horizon each day to hail any ship that might chance to be passing that way.

One day, upon returning from a hunt for food, he was horrified to find his hut in flames! All that he had had now gone up in smoke! The worst had happened, so it appeared. But that which *seemed* to have happened for the worst was, in reality, for the best. To the man's limited vision, it was the worst.

To God's infinite wisdom, his loss was for the best—that for which he had prayed. The very next day a ship arrived. "We saw your smoke signal," the captain said.

Can we not take our seeming calamities, and look for God's best in them?

THE MEANING OF YESTERDAY

Yesterday came with its sunlight and shadows,
    Scattering happiness, fostering strife;
Now with its passing we search for the answer,
    What did our yesterday mean to our life?

Yesterday came with its doubts and its failures,
>Shaking foundations that long held secure;
But in the hush of the night, faith had taught us,
>Only through Christ come the things that endure.

Yesterday came with its sorrows to open
>Deeper and wider the wounds of our heart;
Bitter our anguish, yet clear was its message,
>Life would be feeble had sorrow no part.

Yesterday came with its clouds and its sunshine,
>Weaving together both laughter and tears;
Yet in the twilight we read what was written,
>Yesterdays fit us to master the years.

>—George W. Wiseman

ALL IS WELL

In the centre of the circle
>Of the will of God I stand;
There can come no second causes,
>All must come from his dear hand,
All is well! For 'tis my Father
>Who my life hath planned.

Shall I pass through waves of sorrow?
>Then I know it will be best;
Though I cannot tell the reason,
>I can trust, and so I'm blest.
God is love, and God is faithful,
>So in perfect peace I rest.

With the shade and with the sunshine,
    With the joy and with the pain,
Lord, I trust Thee! Both are needed,
    Each Thy wayward child to train.
Earthly loss, did we but know it,
    Often means our heavenly gain.

—Author unknown

3. CHRISTMAS

THE TRUE MEANING EXPLAINED

The city lies dark and still, with only the tick-tock sound of the huge clock in the church steeple. The long bronze hands on the time-worn face point out the minutes yet to go—four, three, two, one—midnight!

The city has awakened. Candles are lit, voices ring out in joyous unison with the chimes of the grand old clock. 'Tis Christmas, the birthday of Christ the King. One thousand nine hundred and fifty-five years since the night a Virgin Mother gave birth to the Saviour of the world. One thousand nine hundred and fifty-five years since the night a beautiful baby boy lay wrapped in swaddling clothes, snuggled in the hay of the manger with only the breath of the animals to warm His tiny body.

In this present-day world in which Christmas has become so commercialized, we seem often to lose sight of the real meaning. On this Christmas, let us remember that it is Christ's birthday. Let us give Him a pres-

ent of our united efforts to bring peace to this world—
perhaps by finding peace in our own hearts.

How can we do this? By starting today—this
hour, this minute, to love our fellowmen, be they rich
or poor, handsome or homely, genial or grumpy. Love
them no matter what their religion or beliefs. Then,
and only then, will we be able to arrive at peace and
happiness. It isn't such a difficult task if we try.

We think of giving gifts to others on Christ's
birthday. Why not give Him a gift, the best gift ever,
the knowledge that we are at peace with others, and,
consequently, at peace with ourselves.

—M.A.R.
By special permission
Trade School Record
Ahrens Trade School

A CHRISTMAS DAY

The air was still. The angels' song
Had echoed through the sky.
Magi had come a journey long,
And shepherds watched near by.
Time's brightest scroll was there unfurled
Where one small baby lay.
Love was reborn into the world
Upon that Christmas Day.

But even such a lovely thing
Was not enough. That hour
Would swiftly pass, and heaven's King

Must find His throne of power
Within men's lives. There glory starts,
And love—God's gentle way—
Must be reborn in human hearts
To make a Christmas Day.

                    —Clarence Edwin Flynn

No Room for Him

No room for Him,
We grieve that it was so,
And then we go,
Busy upon our way,
With no more courtesy than they
Who turned our Lord away.

Our rooms are full,
There is so much to do,
Each day so new,
I wonder if the Lord of all
Is sad we grant Him space so small,
Less than a manger stall?

                    —Author unknown

The Spirit of Christmas

I question if Christmas can ever be "merry"
     Except to the heart of an innocent child.
For when time has taught us the meaning of sorrow
     And sobered the spirits that once were so wild,
When all the green graves that lie scattered behind us

Like milestones are marking the length of the
way,
And echoes of voices that no more shall greet us
Have saddened the chimes of the bright Christ-
mas day,—
We may not be merry, the long years forbid it,
The years that have brought us such manifold
smarts;
But we may be happy, if only we carry
The Spirit of Christmas deep down in our hearts.

Threefold is the Spirit, thus blending together
The *Faith* of the shepherds who came to the King,
And knowing naught else but the angels' glad mes-
sage,
Had only their faith to His cradle to bring;
The *Hope* of the Wise Men that rose like the day-star
To lighten the centuries' midnight of wrong.
And the *Love* of the Child in the manger low-lying,
So tender and patient, so sweet and so strong.
Hence I shall not wish you the old "Merry Christmas,"
Since that is of shadowless childhood a part,
But one that is *holy* and *happy* and *peaceful*,
The Spirit of Christmas deep down in your heart.

—Annie Johnson Flint

The Carpenter of Syria

Nearly twenty centuries ago there lived in Syria
a humble carpenter, who, in a world that was teeming
with hate, greed, and materialism, went about doing

good to rich and poor alike, urging all men to love one another as they loved themselves, and to do unto others as they would have others do unto them. He also taught the fearful, unwelcome truth that life does not end at the tomb but continues without end, and that "as a man soweth, so shall he reap."

Frenzied with hate and fear when thus dragged face to face with Truth, they put him to death as an enemy of the state and a religious disturber.

Yet of all them who have lived on this planet since the beginning of time, no man is held in higher esteem or greater reverence by the cultured people of the world. The Carpenter of Nazareth, the son of God, taught men how to live!

—The First Baptist Bulletin
Tallahassee, Fla.

4. THE CHURCH

THE CHURCH INVITES YOU TO WORSHIP REGULARLY FOR—

C-leansing

"Though your sins be as scarlet, they shall be as white as snow." It is in the place of prayer that our Saviour's whisper "thy sins are forgiven thee" is most often heard.

H-ealing

"And He healed them." In the days of His flesh, our Lord devoted Himself to a healing ministry. The ills of mind and body and the deeper maladies of the soul yielded to the Master's sovereignty. "His word has still its ancient power." You will find the healing presence of Christ in the house of worship.

U-nifying

"Thy faith hath made thee whole." Psychologists proclaim today that which the church has been saying through the ages—that it is only through committing life to a "power not ourselves" that we can build a strong and unified personality for purposeful living.

R-edeeming

"Ye must be born anew." The church is the medium through which that wondrous miracle of divine grace is wrought and men and women become "new creatures in Christ Jesus."

C-omforting

"Come unto Me all ye that labor and are heavy laden, and I will give you rest." The sense of the Saviour's presence and power, which alone is adequate to lift life's burdens and smooth life's stony roads, is mediated through the hallowed hours in the House of God.

H-eralding

"The Kingdom of God is at hand." The good news of the Kingdom proclaimed through the

church is the one hope of our unhappy world.
It is in the sanctuary that we are moved to dedicate our powers to the building of the Kingdom
of righteousness and peace and love. Through
worship the Christ of history becomes the
Christ of our own experience and we are caught
up in His program of world redemption.

Come Let Us Worship

From *Church Chimes*
Walnut Street Baptist Church
Louisville, Kentucky

THE LITTLE CHURCH

The little church is weather-worn,
    The little church is old;
'Twas built a hundred years ago,
    Or even more, I'm told;
The old bell in the belfry,
    Has rusted out with time,
Yet still it rings on Sunday,
    With an ancient, mellow chime.

A beaten path points the way,
    Where many feet have trod,
But still the people gather there,
    Anon, to worship God;
And if you should ask the question,
    "What faith is held?" they'd say;

"We come to worship Him,
    To bless, to thank, to pray."

The minister is old and gray,
    Some say he's lost his sight;
He moves as if he found his way,
    By some bright, inner light;
He stands before the altar,
    With the Bible in his hand,
While he tells the old, old story
    Of the Saviour of the land.

Behind the church a row of graves
    Are marked, each by a cross,
The little tract is hidden
    By the daisies, grass and moss;
I think Our Father, looking down
    Could hardly help but bless
These kindly souls, in their
    Earnest faithfulness.

—Author unknown
By permission of the Louisville *Courier-Journal*

THE CITY CHURCH

God bless the church on the avenue
That hears the city's cry,
The church that sows the Seed of the Word
Where the masses of men go by;
The church that makes, midst the city's roar,
A place for an Altar of Prayer,

With a heart for the rich—a heart for the poor,
And rejoices their burdens to share.

The church that's true to the call of Christ
Who wept o'er the city's need,
And who sent his disciples to labor for Him
Where the forces of evil breed.
The church that gives and the church that lives
As seen by the Master's eyes—
God bless the church on the avenue
That answers the city's cry.

—Ralph Walker

My Church

My church to me means life;
The more abundant life, enlarged, full-grown;
Unchanging in a swiftly moving age
When hope has flown.

My church to me means love;
An all-embracing love, secure, serene.
With hands outstretched to help the passing throng;
With self unseen.

My church to me means rest;
A quiet, peaceful rest, calm and complete;
Unbroken by the din of worldly strife;
The soul's retreat.

My church to me means home;
A happy, cheerful home, within whose walls

An undivided circle kneels in prayer,
As evening falls.

My church to me means God;
An understanding God who loves His own;
Who woos the sinful and consoles the saint,
When tempest blown.

My church to me means Christ;
A sympathetic Christ, with boundless love,
Who will not rest until each wayward child
Is safe above.

My church to me means hope;
A never failing hope when night descends,
For in that hour it lights the evening lamp
And comfort sends.

My church to me means faith;
Triumphant faith, that clears the cluttered way
Toward that city where for us awaits
Eternal day.

—George W. Wiseman

5. EASTER

AFTERWARD

I shall not die, whatever may befall;
This tent, that shelters for a night
My questioning spirit, may be struck at morn,

When my real pilgrimage begins
Then shall I go.
Like a glad child released from school,
Upon my journey through Eternity,
Leaving my little lesson books
With much unlearned; a tablet with a line
Scrawled childlishly above my name.
(God grant the words ring true
With hope and courage; that I have not cringed
When buffeted by Chance or Fate!)

What then, the great adventure past?
Freed from the bonds of flesh and time and space,
My soul shall rove the universe at will,
Stepping from star to star as once I stepped
From stone to stone across a shallow brook;
Learning creation's secrets; seeing worlds
Made and unmade; learning how lilies seek
And find in black, foul-smelling mire,
Whiteness and fragrance and rare loveliness;
Why robbins sing in rain; why nightingales
Make music in the shadows; why larks soar
To fling their raptures on the upper air.

I shall find work to do—
Helping to poise the rainbows in the sky;
Helping to paint the violet and rose;
Helping a child to mend his broken toy;
Helping the sage to think the thoughts of God;
And I shall grow.

By all I learn, by all I feel and do,
By every thrilling new experience,
Companioning with saints and stars and suns,
With little children and with seraphim,
I shall grow tall of soul, attaining thus
The stature of a joyous child of God.
I shall not die.

—Ida Reed-Smith

Easter Must Be Reclaimed

Easter must be reclaimed.
Too long the world has missed the Easter glow,
Charmed by the glitter of a fashion show,
A dress parade; a gala holiday,
With church-bound manikins upon display.
The faith of Easter never will be caught
By making Christ a fleeting afterthought.

Easter must be redeemed
From revelry that marks the end of Lent,
And worshippers who yearly are content
To journey to God's house, and then forget
That Christ still lives when Easter's sun has set.
The vision fades; the power soon is lost,
If Easter does not lead to Pentecost.

Easter must be relived
Where is the zeal that followed Easter's birth?
The faith that doomed the soulless gods of earth?

No shallow, lifeless spirit of repose
Prevailed that cloudless morn when Christ arose.
The Easter atmosphere cannot revive
A torpid faith that thinks itself alive.

—George W. Wiseman

REVEILLE IN HEAVEN

All the heroes of the nation will be gathered for the
  sight
When the Author of Creation sunders daylight from
  the night,
When the final bugle summons they will gather from
  afar,
He will read out their promotions, pin on each a morn-
  ing star.
And the whirling of the planets will be music of the
  band
When the Universe-Commander takes the great re-
  viewing stand.
There're a thousand from Tarawa, and the gang from
  Kwajelein;
Where the battle-scarred battalions rose from Hill Six
  Hundred Nine.
Here are Merrill's grim Marauders, blood wounds
  washed in morning dew,
There's the valiant St. Lo Major; Wainwright's boys
  pass in review.
Here are boys who held one acre in a skirmish without
  name,

Here is 90007—Heaven knows him just the same!

Rank on rank of marching thousands, tramping over
Heaven's sod,

Captains, privates, sergeants, colonels—all pass equal
before God.

They wear ribbons from the sunset, they wear medals
from the suns,

And the thunder and the lightning flash salute from
Heaven's guns.

They go marching, marching, marching, through the
vistas of the sky—

They go marching on forever—Yankee soldiers never
die!

—Corporal Dana Thomas

Think of Stepping on Shore

Think of stepping on shore
And finding it Heaven;
Think of taking hold of a hand
And finding it God's hand;
Think of breathing new air
And finding it celestial air;
Think of feeling invigorated,
And finding it immortality;
Think of passing from storm to storm,
To an unknown calm;
Think of waking up,
And finding it home.

—Author unknown

THE RISEN CHRIST

The crucified was laid to rest—
    His earthly labors o'er—
In Joseph's own new sepulcher
    Where none had lain before.
Among the people everywhere
    A startling rumor spread
That on the *third day he would rise*
    And live again, though dead!
The High Priest gave authority
    To seal the entrance tight,
And ordered Roman soldiers there
    To watch by day and night.
The Sabbath of the Jews began,
    Then came the second day—
While in the closely-guarded tomb
    His lifeless body lay.
Throughout the watches of the night
    The hours dragged on apace—
The Day of Resurrection dawned—
    An earthquake shook the place!
God's power loosed the bonds of death,
    And through the opened door
The Risen Christ came from the tomb
    To live forevermore!

                    —Author unknown

WALK SLOWLY

If you should go before me, dear, walk slowly
Down the ways of death, well worn and wide,

For I would want to overtake you quickly
And seek the journey's ending by your side.

I would be so forlorn not to descry you
Down some shining highroad when I came;
Walk slowly, dear, and often look behind you
And pause to hear if someone calls your name.

—Adelaide Love

In Memoriam

I watched a sail, it dropped from sight
Over the rounding sea—a gleam of light,
At last, far flashed farewell, and like a thought
Slipt out of mind, it vanished and was not.

Yet, to the helmsman standing at the wheel,
Broad seas still swept before the gliding keel.
Disaster? Change? He left no slightest sign,
Nor dreamed he of that dim horizon line.

So may it be, perchance, when down the tide
Our dear ones vanish. Peacefully they glide
On level seas, nor mark the unknown bound
We call it death—to them 'tis life beyond.

—Selected

Casting All Your Care Upon Him

The skies will darken sometimes,
    Rain clouds gather, too,
But still from out the darkness

The sun will shine through
Our days with grief may darken,
 Sadness may befall,
But behind the loss and darkness
 God's love brightens all.

—Thos. Washbourne

To Comfort You

Others' hearts are heavy
 For the loss that you must bear,
Others', too, are grieving,
 For they understand and care;
Others' prayers are with you . . .
 Fervent prayers that you will know
All the peace and comfort
 That His Presence can bestow.

—Author unknown

There Is a Light to Lead You

There is a light to lead you,
 There is a Love to guide—
There is an Unseen Power
 Forever at your side,
And in this hour of darkness
 A Prayer that you may feel
This life can bring no sorrow
 That Heaven cannot heal.

6. FAITH

FAITH IN OURSELVES

Since the beginning long, long ago at Valley Forge and on Bunker Hill, Americans have had reasons to be proud of their country—and themselves.

From the valleys, the mountains, the plains—from all the States of the Union—they have come to stand wherever blood wrote our history!

And not in war only: But in peace and in the good, clean work of the farm and factory, we have given of ourselves that our nation might prosper.

Americans have cause to be proud—to have faith in themselves.

Sometimes these days, it seems some of us forget the proud company we have joined . . . forget the brave names on monuments where bronze blackens with weather . . . forget the great deeds graven in granite.

Haven't we cause to have faith?

Haven't we the duty to have faith in ourselves—and to let the world know of it?

Each of us can help revive the spirit which built our country—by placing Faith in God . . . in Ourselves . . . in Our Fellow men . . . and in Freedom.

Each of us can help revive the spirit which built our country by keeping these Four Great Faiths and by proclaiming them to the world—not always in words, but surely always in deeds.

—Texas and Pacific
Railroad Company

BEAUTIFUL THINGS

The desire for a fuller, richer life runs as an unbroken thread throughout the history of mankind. This yearning and aspiration to attain perfection is given expression in nearly every object of art. It is the dominant theme in literature and the inspiration of the world's great music. Religion, literature, music—these are the inseparable trinity to which man intuitively turns with faith and confidence for strength to hold a forward course unswervingly through every trial.

It is in these, rather than in the material things, that the spirit finds complete contentment. These irresistible forces alone possess the power to exalt and unify, and have inspired the noblest deeds of valor and sacrifice. However difficult the path, everyone will find courage in the knowledge that the beautiful things in life endure for all time.

—Author unknown

IN GOD WE TRUST
. . . Do We Or Don't We?

Does it mean anything . . . or doesn't it?

Would another phrase do just as well? Our nation's founders didn't think so!

The men who signed the Constitution . . . the men—and women—who braved the prairie and the mountain to pioneer our land . . . they didn't think so.

But what about us? Does this motto on the coin in our pocket guide us . . . strengthen us? Or have we forgotten the power of the faith expressed in these words?

If our country's future is uncertain . . . if we are worried about tomorrow . . . then perhaps the time has come to put aside small things and turn once more to the faiths which made our nation great.

Our country's great leaders down through the years have shared a sure belief in God . . . in themselves . . . in their fellow men . . . and in freedom! In crisis and in peace they have placed their faith in God's wisdom . . . and in their own ability to work out their problems . . . and in the great justice of a free people.

Let us do the same today. For these faiths will renew our strength.

—W. G. Vollmer

A PRAYER FOR FAITH

God, give me back the simple faith that I so long have clung to,

My simple faith in peace and hope, in loveliness and light—

Because without this faith of mine, the rhythms I have sung to

Become as empty as the sky upon a starless night.

God, let me feel that right is right, that reason dwells with reason,

And let me feel that something grows whenever there is rain—

And let me sense the splendid truth that season follows
season,
And let me dare to dream that there is tenderness in
pain.

God, give me back my simple faith because my soul is
straying
Away from all the little creeds that I so long have
known;
Oh, answer me while still I have at least the strength
for praying,
For if the prayer dies from my heart I will be quite
alone.

By permission of Margaret E. Sangster

HOLD THOU MY HAND

Dear Lord,
Hold Thou my hand.
The way is dark
Unless you guide me;
The path is rough
Unless you walk beside me.

Hold Thou my hand;
I do not see the light
That shines above me,
Unless I look into your face
And know that you love me.

And looking up,
I do not mind the stones

That bruise my feet,
The thorns along the path,
Or noontide heat,
For is it not enough to know
That you, My Saviour,
Trod this thorny pathway long ago?
And knowing this,
I'll have no fear
When walking through the darkness
With You near,
For I can look into your face divine
And forward go with my hand in thine.

—Author unknown

My Hand In God's

Each morning when I wake I say,
    "I place my hand in God's today;"
I know He'll walk close to my side
    My every wandering step to guide.

He leads me with the tenderest care
    When paths are dark and I despair—
No need for me to understand
    If I but hold fast to His hand.

My hand in His! No surer way
    To walk in safety through each day.
By His great bounty I am fed;
    Warmed by His love, and comforted.

When at day's end I seek my rest
    And realize how much I'm blessed,
My thanks pour out to Him; and then
    I place my hand in God's again.

—Florence Scripps Kellog

7. HOPE

April Showers

Rain, rain, pouring rain! Bleak gray skies, more rain, wind and cold. Dismal gloomy weather. And then the sun shines forth—bright, fresh, invigorating.

This is April weather. Life is much like that. Days of misgivings and disappointments. Drabness, coldness, bleakness. An inspiring friend comes along with a bit of kindness, an uplifting hand, and like the sun, brightens the entire atmosphere.

One is reminded of the childhood rhyme: "It is not raining rain to me, 'tis raining violets." Which causes us to philosophize with the philosopher that "nothing is drab excepting to the color blind."

Watching the drops of rain fall upon the cold earth one sees and feels only the bleakness of it all. While another sees in each drop of rain a violet, a jonquil, a daffodil, a lily, soon to come forth because the rain softened and nurtured the ground. The rain drops may be diamonds glistening in the sun. Or just muddy water making the walks disagreeable.

April showers are indicative of life and the range

of the scene presented depends much upon the view of the soul.

—Selected

COMFORT AND HOPE

A ship plowed its way down among the cannibalistic islands of the South Seas a number of years ago. On board was a blatant skeptic. The ship was wrecked, and the survivors were washed ashore on an island, where they expected to be eaten. They crept cautiously from the shore up a hill, seeking to discover what lay beyond. At the top, the skeptic suddenly leaped up and shouted, "We are safe, we are safe!" What had he seen? A group of government soldiers? Oh, no. Just a church steeple. He knew the Bible had reached this people first, and he was glad.

Yes, the Bible brings hope, even to the skeptics sometimes.

—From *Strength*

HOPE

So strange and beautiful a thing is hope,
    So infinite its reach, so wide its scope,
For yesterday when I was bent with care,
    With burdens almost more than I could bear,
My heart cried out in bitterness and grief,
    And faith was well-nigh crushed by unbelief;
Then suddenly my spirit knew release,
    In place of doubt I found a lovely peace,
For someone very softly seemed to say,

"Be still and wait—this too will pass away."
I never realized before—how odd—
    That hope is just another word for GOD.

                By permission Marjorie McMahan

8. FRIENDSHIP

WHO IS A FRIEND?

Is there anything more wonderful than a friend,
a real friend, that you are not afraid of imposing upon,
a friend, as the Bible says, "who loveth at all times?"
Such a one will be true, not only when you are prosperous and the future looks bright, but when reverses
come into your life and when all seems to be swept
away. How much we owe to our friends. At the gate-
way of every life, there stands the solitary figure who
has become the inspiration of that life. How much we
owe them! How inconsequential life would be without them. While speaking of friends, remember God
is a friend to us. From jarring discords of selfish greed
and bitter disappointments, He offers peace and lifts
our hearts and eyes toward heaven, from haunting
fears and anxieties, He offers courage and strength,
and when crushing sorrow comes, when it seems the
sun will never shine again, God will be our friend.

            —Chaplain Elbert L. Atkinson, U.S.A.F.

THE HOUSE OF FRIENDSHIP

I have a little world within a world,
    A house of friendship where grief does not fall

Upon my hearth the peaceful kitten, curled,
  Knows that the storm disturbs us not at all.

The shingles of true friendship on my house
  Have made it snug against misfortune's blast,
And though the bitter tempests may carouse,
  My roof is sheltering; my door is fast.

The world outside is huge; my world is not,
  And never does the golden sunshine fade
Upon its lintel . . . constant is the spot
  Where stands the house of friendship we have
    made.

                              —Anne Campbell
                        Reprinted by permission

FRIENDS

Of all the many blessings that our gracious Father
  sends,
I thank Him most of all today for loyal-hearted friends;

Friends who know about my faults and keep on loving
  still,
Friends whose friendship changes not with happy days
  or ill.
Friends to whom my inmost secrets safely I confide,
Friends who make me happy just to have them by my
  side;
Yes! of all the many blessings that our gracious Father
  sends,
I thank Him most of all today for loyal-hearted friends.

I like my friends to meet each other—those for whom
    I care,
I feel their friendship's worth so much I want the rest
    to share;
Friendship's like the miracle of loaves in Galilee,
Though shared by many others, there's none the less
    for me.
And since I've thought of you, dear friend, in friend-
    ship's closest tie,
I've longed to introduce you to a friend, for He and I
Spend many hours together in a happy, solemn tryst,
How I wish that you might know Him! my best Friend,
    Jesus Christ.

                —Rev. Horace G. Halse

THE MAKING OF FRIENDS

If nobody smiled and nobody cheered,
    and nobody helped us along,
If every man looked after himself and
    good things all went to the strong;
If nobody cared just a little for you,
    and nobody thought about me,
And we all stood alone in the battle of life,
    what a dreary old world it would be.
Life is sweet just because of the friends we
    have made and the things in common we share,
We want to live on, not because of ourselves,
    but because of the people who care.
It's giving and doing for somebody else,
    on that all life's splendor depends,

And the joy of the world when you have summed
it all up is found in the making of friends.

—Author unknown

9. GUIDANCE

READ

WHEN in sorrow, read John 14.

WHEN men fail you, Psalm 27.

WHEN you have sinned, Psalm 51.

WHEN you worry, Matthew 6:19–34.

BEFORE church service, Psalm 84.

WHEN you are in danger, Psalm 91.

WHEN you have the blues, Psalm 34.

WHEN God seems far away, Psalm 139.

WHEN you are discouraged, Isaiah 40.

IF YOU DESIRE to be fruitful, John 15.

WHEN doubts come upon you, John 7:17.

WHEN you are lonely or fearful, Psalm 33.

WHEN you forget your blessings, Psalm 103.

FOR JESUS' idea of a Christian, Matthew 5.

FOR JAMES' idea of religion, James 1:19–27.

FOR STIRRING of faith, Hebrews 11.

WHEN you feel down and out, Romans 8:31–39.

WHEN you lack courage for your task, Joshua 1.

WHEN the world seems bigger than God, Psalm 90.

WHEN you want Christian assurance, Romans 8:1–30.

WHEN you leave home for labor or travel, Psalm 121.

WHEN you grow bitter or critical, I Cor. 13.

FOR PAUL'S idea of Christianity, II Cor. 5:15–19.

FOR PAUL'S RULES on how to get along with men, Romans 12.

—Selected

IF YOU STAND VERY STILL

If you stand very still in the heart of a wood,
You will hear many wonderful things—
The snap of a twig and the wind in the trees,
And the whir of invisible wings.

If you stand very still in the turmoil of life,
And you wait for the voice from within,
You'll be led down the quiet ways of wisdom and peace
In a mad world of chaos and din.

If you stand very still and you hold to your faith
You will get all the help that you ask;
You will draw from the Silence the things that you
     need—
Hope and Courage and Strength for your task.

—Author unknown

TOMORROW

The love of God has hung a veil
     Around tomorrow,
That we may not its beauty see,
     Nor trouble borrow.
But, oh, 'tis sweeter far, to trust
     His unseen Hand,
And know that all the path of life

His wisdom planned.
I know not if tomorrow's way
    Be steep, or rough;
But when His hand is guiding me,
    That is enough.
And so, although the veil has hid
    Tomorrow's way,
I walk with perfect faith and trust
    Through each today!

—H. H. Pentney

Self Dependence

Weary of myself and sick of asking
    What I am and what I ought to be
At this vessel's prow I stand, which bears me
    Forwards, forwards, o'er the starlit sea.

And a look of passionate desire
    O'er the sea and to the stars I send:
"Ye who from my childhood up have calmed me,
    Calm me, Oh, compose me to the end!

From the intense clear, star sown vault of heaven
    Over the lit sea's unquiet way
In the rustling night air came the answer;
    "Woulds't thou be as these are: LIVE as they.

"Unaffrighted by the silence round them,
    Undistracted by the sights they see
These demand not that the things without them
    Yield them love, amusement, sympathy.

"And with joy the stars perform their shining,
    And the sea its long, moon-silver'd roll;
For self-poised they live, nor pine with noting
    All the fever of some differing soul.

"Bounded by themselves, and unregardful
    In what state God's other works may be,
In their own tasks all their powers pouring,
    These attain the mighty life you see."

O air-borne voice! long since, severely clear,
    A cry like thine in mine own heart I hear:
"Resolve to be thyself; and know that he
    Who finds himself, loses his misery!"

                    —Matthew Arnold

10. KINDNESS

GETTING EVEN

It is amazing and astonishing! It is a marvelous miracle and it is a miraculous marvel! The Christian has a way to "get even" when unkind, keen, cutting evil is done against him. It is to use kindness to counteract and immune against unkindness. When God declares, "Be ye kind one to another," he states a principle that carries out the more blessed to give than to receive philosophy, but also He states a practical principle for the practitioner of Christ. The Apostle Paul states that to be kind to the unkind person is the keen way of getting even, for in so doing it "heaps coals of fire on his head." It works into his thinking, it works on his mind until warmed therein he thinks, "This fellow has been kind to me even though I have been unkind, therefore I must be his friend, I do not agree with all he says or does but I must be his friend."

That is the Christian getting even for he evens up the gap between himself and the other person with the magnetic drawing power which never fails—he is living like Jesus lived. The unkind person can resist unkindness, hate and selfishness for he has these in his heart, but the unkind person cannot resist keen, undeserved kindness.

—George H. Riggs

A Smile

A smile costs nothing but gives much—
It takes but a moment, but the memory of it usually
    lasts forever.
None are so rich that can get along without it—
And none are so poor but that can be made rich by it.
It enriches those who receive
Without making poor those who give—
It creates sunshine in the home,
Fosters good will in business
And is the best antidote for trouble—
And yet it cannot be begged, borrowed or stolen, for
    it is of no value
Unless it is freely given away.
Some people are too busy to give you a smile—
Give them one of yours—

For the good Lord knows that no one needs a smile so
    badly
As he or she who has no more smiles left to give.

—Author unknown

BE CAREFUL WHAT YOU SAY

In speaking of a person's faults,
    Pray don't forget your own;
Remember those with homes of glass
    Should seldom throw a stone.

If we have nothing else to do
    But talk of those who sin
'Tis better we commence at home,
    And from that point begin.

Some may have faults—and who has not?
    The old as well as young—
Perhaps we may, for aught we know,
    Have fifty to their one.

I'll tell you of a better plan.
    You'll find it works full well.
To try my own defects to cure
    Before of others tell.

And though I sometimes hope to be
    No worse than some I know,
My own shortcomings bid me let
    The faults of others go.

Then let us all when we commence
    To slander friend or foe
Think of the harm one word would do
    To those we little know.

Remember, curses sometimes, like
    Our chickens, "roost at home,"
Don't speak of others' faults until
    We have none of our own.

—Anonymous

How to Begin a Month

Everyone has had the experience of waking up to the bright sunlight of a spring morning and thinking suddenly, "This is the first of May;" opening one's eyes to the crispness of an autumn dawn and saying, "The beginning of October!"

We can at the beginning of the month, set out with the will to clear away the debris of our lives, the routine of habits and lethargies, our deadnesses to the world. For it is we, not the world, who have grown drab.

Today, start to keep your eye on the world, not on yourself, and see how many of your little personal anxieties will roll away. Start the gesture of friendliness and neighborliness you had intended. If you are multiplied by millions, you will have gone a long way toward a democratic world . . . a month of such behavior itself will be so rewarding you will be less torn with anxiety about the future. . . .

A month is not a long time . . . we can begin now

acting as if this were the last month in history, and acting also as if this were the first month in which we are really living. . . . By the end of the month we shall be both happier and more useful. A weary young woman once said to her colleagues in an office, "I'm tired of living." A buoyant friend replied, "Have you tried it yet?" It is the beginning of the month. It is time to begin. Rome was not built in a day. But we have thirty days. Wars have been won in less, lives made over.

—Irwin Edman

To Be Desired

Are you willing to stoop down and consider the needs and the desires of little children; to remember the weakness and loneliness of people who are growing old; to stop asking how much your friends love you, and ask yourself whether you love them enough; to bear in mind the things what those who live in the same house with you really want, without waiting for them to tell you; to trim your lamp so that it will give more light and less smoke, and to carry it in front so that your shadow will fall behind you; to make a grave for your ugly thoughts, and a garden for your kindly feelings, with the gate open?

—Henry Van Dyke

Give Me the Love of Friends

Give me the love of friends, and I
Shall not complain of cloudy sky,

Or little dreams that fade and die.
Give me the clasp of one firm hand,
The lips that say, "I understand,"
And I shall walk on holy land.
For fame and fortune burdens bring,
And winter takes the rose of spring;
And friendship is a Godlike thing!

—Anonymous

11. LIFE

Why a River Becomes Crooked

Did you ever see a river that was straight as an arrow? Probably not. They generally wind back and forth from the time they gush out of a mountain spring or seep out of a lake until they find repose in the bosom of the great deep.

And why is it that the river is never straight?

Let a master of epigram answer and at the same time drive home a wholesome truth: "A river becomes crooked by following the line of least resistance! So does man!"

—Selected

Life's Greatest Dimension

Life's greatest dimension is the one that lies just beyond. The lure of the unrealized is the subtle urge which has made man a seeker, a dreamer, an inventor, an explorer upon the face of the earth. Life's meaning is never determined by past achievements alone, but by the degree in which we respond to the appeal of what might be.

How we need to understand that it is our sacred privilege to hasten the future through some deed of our own, and to realize it through our devotion! Time-creatures are we with the ability of gods, endowed with the power to mold infinite, shapeless possibilities to our hearts' desires. Each of us may become the creator of something better which still sleeps in the realm of the beyond!

—W. Waldemar W. Argow

GET SOMETHING DONE

Get something done; the golden hours
    Are passing swiftly on,
Invest your heaven-given powers
    Before the chance is gone.
Don't ask the world to entertain;
    Serve it while you can.
Above all else, do not complain;
    Do something! Be a man!

The day will end, the night will fall,
    And leave you gay or sad.
The world will cease to care at all
    How good a time you had.
The artificial things will be
    Forgot at set of sun.

Who then will live on in memory?
    He who got something done.

                —Clarence Edwin Flynn

IT'S IN YOUR FACE

You don't have to tell how you live each day,
    You don't have to say if you work or you play,
A tried, true barometer serves in the place—
    However you live, it will show in your face.
The false, the deceit, that you bear in your heart
    Will not stay inside where it first got the start;
For sinew and blood are thin veil of lace—
    What you wear in your heart you wear in your
        face.
If you have gambled and won in the great game of life,
    If you feel you have conquered the sorrow and
        strife,
If you've played the game fair and you stand on first
        base—
    You don't have to say so, it shows on your face.
If your life is unselfish, and for others you live,
    For not what you get, but how much you can give.
If you live in good will toward the whole human race,
    You don't have to tell it—it shows in your face.

                —Masonic Home Journal

LIFE

Let me but live life from year to year,
    With forward face and unreluctant soul;

Not hurrying to, nor turning from the goal;
>Not mourning for the things that disappear
In the dim past, nor holding back in fear
>From what the future veils: but with a whole
And happy heart that pays its toll
>To YOUTH and AGE, and travels on with cheer.
So let the way wind up the hill or down.
>O'er rough or smooth, the journey will be joy;
Still seeking what I sought when but a boy,
>New friendship, high adventure, and a crown
My heart will keep the courage of the quest,
>And hope the road's last turn will be the best.

—Henry Van Dyke

My Symphony

To live content with small means; to seek elegance rather than luxury, refinement rather than fashion; to be wealthy, not rich, to study hard, think quietly, talk gently, act frankly; to listen to stars and birds, to babes and sages with open heart; to bear all cheerfully, do all bravely, await occasions, never hurry. In a word, to let the spiritual unbidden and unconscious grow up thru the common. This is to be my symphony.

—Wm. Henry Channing

His Way Is Best

I may not always know the way,
>Wherein God leads my feet;

But this I know, that round my path,
    His love and wisdom meet.
And so I rest, content to know,
    He guides my feet wher'ere I go.

O, Precious peace within my heart;
    O blessed rest to know
A Father's love keeps constant watch
    Amid life's ebb and flow;
I ask no more than this; I rest content
    And know his way is best.

from *Strength*

12. LIVING

WHO REALLY LIVES?

When do we live? How gauge and measure living? These are big questions with amazing and many counterfeit answers from the world. The world is seldom right in answering. For example, there lived a famous and famed man . . . when his name was mentioned, all bowed in allegiance. He lived in pomp and power. One of his flowery banquets to entertain one hundred courtiers of his kingdom cost $32,000.00. The world said, "Long live Nero the Great." In that same country lived a man named . . . let's see, what was his name? . . . Oh, yes—Paul.

He was in a dirty, dingy dungeon . . . chained and starved. The world said when it tried Paul, "He is a man made mad by too much learning." He is crazy to follow Jesus of Nazareth . . . for it has gotten him excluded from his family, expelled from his tribe and excommunicated from his race. That, the world said then . . . Long live Nero, kill Paul. But how different time has proved it. Nero? What do you know about him? The one thing the most of us think we know about Nero is not true . . . that he sat on the wall and played his fiddle while Rome burned and that is not true, for there were no fiddles then. But—Paul? Paul, the Christian is known and loved the world over. Loved by Jew and Gentile. So if you have a little baby boy born in your family, you affectionately name that little boy Paul. When that little boy becomes about three years of age, you give him a little dog and you name the pup . . . Nero. Who really lived, Paul or Nero?

—George H. Riggs

Let's Try This

Goethe, the master mind of the German people, said: "A man should hear a little music, read a little poetry, and see a fine picture every day of his life in order that worldly cares may not obliterate the sense of the beautiful which God has implanted in the human soul.

The music may be the notes of a bird, the voice of a friend; the poetry may be in stones, or in the breath of spring thru the naked boughs of the trees; the picture may be a sunrise, or a sunset; the outline of a boat at sea, or the silhouette of a man at the plow.

Out of real living a man may hear music, read poetry and see a fine picture every day."

—Selected

The Leadership of Love

If I allow the sordid things
  Of life to press
Me to their bosom without sign
  Of inward stress,
My actions tell, however suave
  My words might be,
That what I love has claimed not part,
  But most of me.

If I bestow on greed or gold
  Approving nods,
I then confess that I adore
  Earth's lifeless gods,
And worship them, no matter what
  I might disclaim,
Accepting God, not with my heart,
  But just in name.

But if I yield myself to Christ
  And with each day,
Give unto Him the love that earth
  Now takes away,
His will would then be my concern,
  For this I know,

That where I place my love, there too,
    My heart will go.

—George W. Wiseman

A DAY OF QUIETUDE

It would not be at all amiss if we
Took one whole day to live deliberately;
To leave the ceaseless whirl and seek a lane
And walk its peaceful, shadowed length again,
With thoughts attuned to nature's growing things—
To hear the feathers of thrushes' wings;
To stand in silence by a gentle stream,
Unruffled by a vague or fretful scheme;
To hearken to the whisper of the grass
As over it the playful breezes pass,
To bring our scattered selves to bear until
We really see the sky beyond the hill.
To have an evening meal with prayerful grace,
To note the smile upon a loved one's face,
To give attention to a spoken word
And try to show that we have truly heard,
To gain a calm in which to hear a sage
Speak from the frame of some old classic's page,
And underneath the sprinkle of the stars
Look upward from the earth and all its scars,
We would face days ahead in better mood
For living one bright day in quietude.

—Reid Crowell

13. MIRACLES

WHAT IS A MIRACLE?

Webster defines a miracle as "an event or effect contrary to the established conditions and courses of things; a supernatural event." The Bible's idea of a miracle would go farther than that, and add the words, "from moral ends," or something similar. The work of the devil might be supernatural and yet not a miracle. Anything is supernatural that is above nature's regular laws or above man's power. But a miracle has the moral element in it. It is a work higher than nature, or higher than man for some moral or Divine purpose.

Belief in miracles depends on belief in God. Of course atheists reject miracles; so do pantheists and deists. But if God has personality, will, and intelligence, surely it is easy to believe that He can perform the miraculous. The incarnation and resurrection of Christ were God's greatest miracles, but it is a miracle today when a life is transformed, and a soul is born again by the power of God's Spirit. The Lord works this miracle, and others, in response to our faith in him.

—W. C. Boone

A QUIET PLACE

The trail down from the mine was very rough. Scores of hobnailed boots had scarred it beyond repair. Thistles fringed it and rattlesnakes were a constant menace. It was easy enough to climb in the morning when one was fresh but when it had lain under the blazing sun all day it was rugged going. And I dreaded it.

But there was one comfort that made up for the blistered heels and thorny scratches. After you rounded the big oak the little meadow lay before you, serene and cool. And all the bitter sweat of the day fell from you at the sight of its loveliness.

It was not a famous scene. Just a smooth bit of grass, spangled with daisies and buttercups, with a tiny stream lisping its way through the weeds. But in some strange way it healed the soul. One forgot the drudgery and dreariness of the day with all its small irritations and entered into a place of peace.

And when I left that little place I was quite a different person. The edge had been rubbed off me by some gentle magic. I had forgotten my gripes and frets. The very earth seemed softer, more yielding.

Remembering that quiet miracle, I often think how different life might be for all of us if we had a quiet place like that somewhere within our spirits, a place where we could leave behind all the nagging worries, harsh fears, and rasping regrets and walk for just a little while—in peace. It would be a little like walking with God—wouldn't it?

—Elsie Robinson

YOU DON'T BELIEVE IN MIRACLES?

"He shall cover thee with His pinions. . . ." Down through the years of man's travail on this earth, the

winged messengers of heaven have come to his deliverance whenever he called for help in faith, believing. So often has this happened that wings have become the symbol of God's love and care for His children.

When Elijah went into hiding from his enemies,
God sent the ravens to feed him. When for many days
Noah was stranded on Mt. Ararat, a dove cooed in his
ear and he was answered. Help had come. . . .

These stories are dimmed in the mists of time
and they have passed into our speech as symbols. . . .
Our light reference to these miracles implies that.
The prophets are dead; there is no direct and personal
communication to be had with God; the day of miracles is over. Are we so sure?

You don't believe in miracles? They abound. You,
a human being, are a miracle nobody has ever been
able to explain save as a work of God. The airplane is
a miracle.

Man groped his way toward the celestial beauty
in life through work. He found his wings, and now
soars in the sky.

Let us pray for yet another miracle: That man,
on wings as the ravens and the dove, may carry God's
love, mercy and peace to suffering men throughout the
world.

—Angelo Patri

A Package of Seed

I paid a dime for a package of seed
And the clerk tossed them out with a flip

We've got 'em assorted for every man's needs
He said with a smile on his lips
Pansies, and poppies and astors and peas
Ten cents a package and pick as you please.

Now seeds are just dimes to the man in the store
And the dimes are the things that he needs
And I've been to buy them in seasons before
But have thought of them merely as seeds.
But it flashed thru my mind as I took them this time
You have purchased a miracle here for a dime.

You've a dimes worth of power which no man can
    create
You've a dimes worth of life in your hand
You've a dimes worth of mystery, destiny, fate,
Which the wisest cannot understand.
In this bright little package, now isn't it odd
You've a dimes worth of something known only to
    God.

These are seeds, but the plants and the blossoms are
    here
With their petals of various hues
In these little pellets so dry and so queer
There is power which no chemist can fuse,
Here is one of God's miracles soon to unfold
Thus for ten cents an ounce is divinity sold.

                        —Author unknown

May Blossoming

All of the storm clouds blew away.
April is passed and it is May.
Where March winds brushed the apple trees,
Blossoms are greeting the springtime breeze,
Daffodils, slices of warm gold sun,
Gleam in the fields where the children run.

Nature is kind in the sunny May,
Blowing the winter storms away;
Carpeting all the ground with green
Giving us beauty where blight has been;
Lavishly sending blue skies and flowers
To make us forget the winter hours.

If we can read it, the lesson's plain,
After our sorrow, joy comes again;
Never a tragedy time cannot ease . . .
As nature gives leaves to the barren trees
So do God's healing angels bring
To the stricken heart, fresh blossoming.

—Ann Campbell
Reprinted by permission

14. MOTHER AND HOME

Memories of Home

The words "mother" and "home" have a magic
appeal, the most sacred recollections and memories of
our childhood days. In the home, mother is a symbol

of deep affection to the family circle, courage, patience, happiness, hopefulness; our mothers reared and nurtured us and made home a dear haven of peace and joy. Home is the laugh of the baby, the song of a mother, the strength of a father, warmth of loving hearts, lights from happy eyes, kindness, loyalty, comradeship. Home is the first school and the first church of the young. Home is where they go for comfort when they are hurt or sick; where joy is shared and sorrow eased; where fathers and mothers are respected and loved; where children are wanted; where money is not so important as loving kindness; where even the teakettle sings from happiness. That is home— God bless it.

—Chaplain Elbert L. Atkinson, U.S.A.F.

Happy He With Such a Mother

I loved her; one
Not learned, save in gracious household ways,
Nor perfect, nay, but full of tender wants;
No angel, but a dearer being, all dipt
In angel instincts, breathing Paradise,
Interpreter between the gods and men,
Who looked all native to her place and yet
On tiptoe seemed to touch upon a sphere
Too gross to tread, and all male minds perforce
Swayed to her from their orbits as they moved
And girdled her with music. Happy he
With such a mother; faith in womankind

Beats with his blood, and trusts in all things high
Come easy to him, and though he trip and fall,
He shall not blind his soul with clay.

—Alfred Tennyson

BEATITUDES FOR THE HOME

Blessed are they who rejoice in their children;
To them is revealed the Fatherhood of God.
Blessed are they who know the power of love;
They dwell in God, for God is love.
Blessed are the songful of soul;
They carry light and joy to shadowed lives.
Blessed are they who see visions;
They shall rejoice in the hidden ways of God.
Blessed are they that have understanding hearts,
For them shall be multiplied kingdoms of delight.
Blessed are the childless, loving children still;
Theirs shall be a mightier family—even as the stars of
    heaven.
Blessed are they whose memories we cherish;
Our thoughts and jewels to their crowns.

—John Oxenham

DOORS

Some doors have hearts, it seems to me,
They open so invitingly;
You feel they are quite kind—akin,
To all the warmth you find within.

Some doors, so weather beaten, grey,
Swing open in a listless way,
As if they wish you had not come.
Their stony silence leaves you dumb.

Some classic doors stand closed and barred,
As if their beauty might be marred
If any sought admittance there,
Save king or prince or millionaire.

Oh, may mine be a friendly door;
May all who cross the threshold o'er,
Within, find sweet content and rest,
And know each was a welcome guest.

—Lona MacDorman
in *The Religious Telescope*

15. NATURE

OCTOBER

Summer is gone; and like a robe, dropped from the shoulders of a dancer in some flashing roundelay, the shimmer of October silences falls upon the land, and all is still.

The sanguine struggle of summer is ended. There is no more mating, no more growing, no more reaching upward. Even the sap has ceased to flow. Life is at the flood, the ebb-tide, ere long, begins, and then the earth, for very need of rest, will lie in the warm sun and dream.

All about us are the silences, and the lonely

sounds—the caw of the crow, the chirp of the cricket, the long rows of fodder, the leaves that, one by one, go to make their beds with other leaves, long gone before; the whole earth is like a great concert hall now closed. These last sounds echo like the final strains of a grand symphony.

October is a mood, and one can scarcely fail to enter into its sorrow, a sorrow that is not the lament of death; for October is "the sunset of the seasons, the preparation of another dawn."

—Barton Rees Pogue

Trees in Autumn

How beautiful in autumn are the trees,
　　Lifting up to God their wistful hands!
How soothing are their calm philosophies—
　　Untroubled trees, amid the troubled lands.
Trees of autumn have the kindest word,
　　For all who pass their still, enchanted ways,
And whispering the tales our fathers heard,
　　We learn how fair the old, immortal days.
The trees, I fancy, sense the season's end,
　　For then they put their brightest garments on;
With mortals' moods how well their colors blend,
　　Ere down the vale the broken leaves are blown,
The trees are holy temples where our feet
　　Go wand'ring still for vanished deities;
On hill or dale or by the noisy street,
　　How beautiful in autumn are the trees!

By permission of J. T. Potts

THE APPLE-BLOSSOM MOON

The apple-blossom moon is shining now
Above the orchard's petaled trees,
Sending its silver radiance to the bough;
Weaving enchanted harmonies.

The birds are silent in the fragrant night
The heavens hold one pure white star,
The apple-blossom moon is shining bright,
Shedding its mystic light afar.

Here is fulfillment of the ancient pledge
Of spring to hearts that need a boon;
Spilling its happy splendor, from the edge
Of Heaven, comes the apple-blossom moon.

—Ann Campbell
Reprinted by permission

QUESTION

God has given me
So many lovely things;
Gulls dipping in the sea,
With swift, sun-silvered wings;
Ripe fruit and golden grain;
Tall mountain peaks, cool glades;
Trees lifted in the rain;
Sunsets of changing shades.

God's gifts to me
No time or tide can stem,

For they are free,
What have I given him?

—Pauline Tyson Stephens

16. THE NEW YEAR

CHRISTIAN ATTITUDE FOR THE NEW YEAR

The New Year always suggests the comparison of the old and the new. Jesus' parable of the householder (Matthew 13:52) teaches that there is value in both. A Christian disciple, a learner in the school of Christ, is compared with a householder who brings out of his treasures, things both new and old. It is a picture of a wealthy man bringing out of his storehouse and distributing to his servants, garments or supplies, some recently acquired, some which he had had on hand for some time, using wisdom and care in the distribution of both classes of goods. Both the new and the old would have their use. He did not use only old things and fail to provide himself with new supplies as needed, nor did he discard all the old and make exclusive use of new things. So it is with a man who is a follower of Christ.

There are three attitudes that men take with reference to the old and the new. The conservatives say, "The old is best, let us not change anything." The radical says, "The new is best, let us change everything." The proper attitude for the Christian is, "There is good in both the old and the new. Let us prove all things, hold fast that which is good."

It would be well if we would make a New Year resolution to carry out this correct Christian attitude.

—W. C. Boone

THE NEW YEAR

I am the New Year, and I come to you pure and un-
    stained,
Fresh from the hand of God.
Each day, a precious pearl to you is given
That you must string upon the silver thread of Life.
Once strung can never be unthreaded but stays
An undying record of your faith and skill.
Each golden minute link you then must weld into the
    chain of hours
That is no stronger than its weakest link.
Into your hands is given all the wealth and power
To make your life just what you will.
I give to you free and unstinted, twelve glorious
    months
Of soothing rain and sunshine golden;
The days for work and rest, the nights for peaceful
    slumber.
All that I have I give with love unspoken.
All that I ask—you keep the faith unbroken!

—J. D. Templeton

BUILDING A NEW YEAR

I would build a new year, Lord,
    Of shining, golden days;

A year that leaves the hallowed marks
    Of Spirit on earth's ways.
I would put into each day's hours
    Those thoughts and words and deeds
Which are the outflow of a mind
    That on Thy substance feeds.
Oh, I would build a year of days
    Alive with love and prayer;
A year wherein no wishings vain
    Or dust of dreams will share.
The light of Truth shall be my guide
    Throughout the year I make;
For I would build as Christ directs
    And for His own name's sake.

—Elizabeth Ross

What Makes a New Year New?

What makes a New Year new?
Not ringing bells or changing dates,
For these soon cease, but not the weights
Of tyranny or lust and greed
On which small men and nations feed;
The world grows big when love controls
Its grasping, hardened, shrunken souls,
This makes a New Year new.

What makes a New Year new?
Not smug contentment with the past,
The mold in which earth's wrongs are cast;
But prophets, unafraid, alive,

To match the age; great souls who strive
To furnish for man's highest good
True justice, peace, and brotherhood.
This makes a New Year new.

What makes a New Year new?
Not resolutions lightly made,
Or worthless dreams born but to fade;
But faith in Christ instead of fate,
More room for God and less for hate;
The world receives its second birth
When God through Christ controls the earth.
This makes a New Year new.

—George W. Wiseman

17. PRAYER

A Morning Prayer

The day returns and brings us the petty round of irritating duties. Help us to play the man, help us to perform them with laughter and smiling faces. Let cheerfulness abound with industry. Give us to go blithely on our business all the day, and bring us to our resting beds weary and content and unashamed and grant us in the end the gift of sleep. Amen.

—Robert Louis Stevenson

A Happy Day

Today will be a happy day
If, first, you find some time to pray;

If, first, alone you go apart
From worldly things, and in your heart
You make resolve to do your best
And then to God you leave the rest.
For God will take the hate and fear
Of yesterday and yesteryear
And in their place, He'll make you feel
The light and love He would reveal
Yes, this will be a happy day
If, friend, right now you'll stop and pray.

—Author unknown

A PRAYER FOR TEACHERS

As to the seer in ancient time
The angel came with coal of flame,
And touched his lips that he might speak,—
O God, in thine Almighty name,
So to us in this later day
Send down a purifying ray.

Put forth thy hand and touch our mouths
Whose holy task it is to teach
And guide the minds of eager youth,
That we may have inspiring speech,
Grant us vast patience, insight wise,
The open mind and heart and eyes.

Thus cleansed and quickened may we go
And teach those in the morn of life—
The beauty and the might of peace,

The sin and ugliness of strife.
Then shall the angel voice proclaim,
"You, too, have spoken in God's name."

—Marguerite Emilio

A Teacher Prays

Before this class I stand as teacher, Lord;
I am responsible for them today,
This is a fearful task, and I am weak;
Oh, guide me, Father, tell me what to say.

Each pupil has the right to find in me
A teacher worthy of respect and trust;
I would not fail this confidence of theirs,
I would be faithful to them—Lord, I must.

It is the privilege of every one
To look to me for guidance—this I know,
I must be careful lest my feet should stray;
They are so apt to follow where I go.

They listen and believe the things I say,
I pray that thou wilt fill my words with power,
Help me to teach with earnestness and truth,
This is a holy and a sacred hour.

Before this class I stand as teacher, Lord;
Mine is a mighty and God-given task;
No recompense of glory or reward,
But grace to teach aright is all I ask.

—By permission of Marjorie McMahan

YOUTH'S PRAYER

To build a life that's clean, upright, secure,
God's Temple that will through the years endure;
To walk courageously, steadfast and sure;
This is my prayer.

To dedicate my life, my youth, my all
To Christ, and then in answer to His call,
Be faithful to each task—the large, the small;
This is my prayer.

—George W. Wiseman

A MOTHER'S PRAYER

I thank Thee for this child of mine—
    This precious gift of Love Divine,
Whom Thou has trusted to my care;
    My heart o'erflows with praise and pray'r.

In faith, Dear Lord, I humbly ask,
    Help me be faithful to my task;
May Thy great grace flow out through me,
    That I may lead my child to Thee.

Oh, grant me wisdom, patience, love,
    From Thine own fullness, Lord above,
That I may understanding be,
    And teach my child to live for Thee.

    And hold it, as Thou holdest mine;
Lord, take her little hand in Thine,

E'er lead her, as Thou leadest me,
And keep her always close to Thee.

—Margaret K. Fraser
from *Strength*

18. PROMISES OF GOD

Count Your Blessings

As I walked through the rain I bundled my raincoat closer around me to keep out the drops. The earth, on the other hand, was eagerly soaking up every bit and the green grass, as if offering thanksgiving to the Giver, was pushing its way skyward. "How much like people," I thought, "for the Promises of God, like the rain, are falling on us all." But some will choose to draw their coat of indifference, of pride, of skepticism, (the coat is of many materials) more closely about them and keep the promises out. And some will eagerly take them in, counting each as a blessing.

For just as rain drops are too numerous to count, so are the Promises of God. But only as we accept the One Great Promise will we recognize the others for what they are.

God fulfilled His Promise upon a cross. Jesus Christ is the focus for our lives. As the grass receives life from the rain, so we who drink of this living water shall never thirst.

—Conrad Crow

God Hath Not Promised

God hath not promised
    Skies always blue,
Flower-strewn pathways
    All our lives through;
God hath not promised
    Sun without rain,
Joy without sorrow,
    Peace without pain.

But God hath promised
    Strength for the day
Rest for the labor,
    Light for the way,
Grace for the trials,
    Help from above,
Unfailing sympathy,
    Undying love.

           —Annie Johnson Flint

The Hill

As I stood in the morn, at the foot of the hill,
    With my spirit forlorn, unresigned to His will—
"Oh, dear Lord," I did cry, "I'm so weary today,
    And the hill is so high—is there no other way?"
Then my Shepherd replied, "though the pathway be
      steep,
    I'll be close by your side, and your feet I will
      keep.

I'll be holding your hand, and your strength I'll sup-
ply,
    Till at even you stand on the hill-top so high."

So together we went, with His hand upon mine,
    And I found sweet content in his presence divine.
Then my pathway seemed bright, as we traveled
along,
    For my spirit grew light, and my heart filled with
song.
At the close of the day, on the summit I stood,
    Looking down at the way, where my Shepherd
so good
Had been leading me on; and it seemed not so steep
    As it had at the dawn, nor the valleys so deep;
For He leveled the road, step by step, as He led,
    And where dangers abode, he was always ahead.

So I learned on the hill, as I stood at the crest,
That to walk in His Will is the way that is best.

                —M.K.F.
            from *Strength*

19. A TEACHER'S RESPONSIBILITY

JESUS, THE MASTER TEACHER

The two-fold task of the teacher is to guide the
spiritual and intellectual growth of his students "to

mature manhood, to the measure of the stature of the fulness of Christ." His aim is the development of saintliness and scholarship in each of his students. Thus, the true teacher does more than merely impart knowledge. He imparts information plus inspiration. In short, he aims at the development of the whole person.

The teacher confronts his students with reality and stimulates them to explore for themselves the mysteries of human existence and the universe. . . . True learning is more than the mere pursuit of truth. It involves the translation of truth into everyday living, for the elimination of every form of injustice, and for the promotion of human welfare.

Three conditions are necessary for the development of such persons. These elements were employed by Jesus, the Master Teacher. They are fellowship, objectivity, freedom of thought, and personal example. Jesus created a fellowship of learning among His disciples. He stimulated His students to think for themselves. He taught in such a way as to lead His disciples to form positive convictions and inspired them to act upon them. Finally, Jesus embodied in His personality the ideals which He sought to infuse in the personalities of His pupils. These are the principles which every effective teacher must lay to heart. For these were the methods and principles of Jesus, the greatest of teachers.

—H. H. Barnette

A Teacher's Prayer

Lord, give me not just words to say,
    Though I need just right words, too,
But strength to live in such a way
    My life will make my words ring true.

Then give me all the sure finesse
    An artist has who blends
Two colors so no one can guess,
    Where one begins, the other ends!

                —Jessie Merle Franklin

In the Heart of a Child

Train up a child in the way he should go; and when he is old, he will not depart from it.
                —Proverbs 22:6

An angel paused in his onward flight
With a seed of love, and truth, and right,
And said: "Oh, where can this seed be sown
That it yield more fruit when fully grown?
To whom can this precious seed be given
That it may bear most fruit for earth and heaven?"
The Saviour heard and said, as He smiled,
"Place it at once in the heart of a child."
The angel whispered the blessed truth
To a weary teacher of precious youth;
Her face grew bright with heavenly light
As she led their thoughts in the way of right.

                —Author unknown

Lest I Forget

Lest I forget to do the things
That give to others peace and joy;
Lest I forget to guide aright
Some mother's careless, wayward boy,
O God, increase the spark of love
That burns within this soul of mine
That I may find the perishing,
And lead them to Thy holy shrine.
Lest I forget to freely give
Of all I have received from Thee;
Lest I forget the cry of need
That comes from darkened lands to me,
Oh keep my heart in tune with Thine,
Lift me from self and into Thee,
That I may hear and see and feel,
The heartbreaks of humanity.

—Corann Pearson

20. REVERENCE

Kinship with Him

Reverence has a special meaning for Christians that is not found in other religions. The word originally meant "fear" and "falling down," and for most of the peoples of the world, worship has meant little more than that. What a tragedy that throughout the history of the world most of mankind has bowed down in fear and trembling before cruel and unknown gods.

Sometimes, in their great desire to get the approval of these horrible deities, men have indulged in human sacrifice. The blood-stained altars of the ancient Aztecs of Mexico give us enough understanding of the hopelessness of pagan religions.

But for the Christian, reverence is something quite different. Christ said, "Our Father . . . hallowed be Thy name." For the first time in human history God was called Father. What a great difference this makes! We Christians, too, bow head and heart to God and acknowledge our submission and inferiority to Him, but we bow down in hope! God is our Father, and we can joyfully claim kinship with Him. He is a loving father to be worshiped, loved, respected, and obeyed. In our reverence we recognize our own inferiority and His great majesty, but we also bind ourselves closer to our Heavenly Father who is ever willing to comfort and guide His own.

—Carl Fields

'MID ALL THE TRAFFIC OF THE WAYS

'Mid all the traffic of the ways,
Turmoils without, within;
Make in my heart a quiet place,
And come and dwell within.

—John Oxenham

DROP THY STILL DEWS OF QUIETNESS

Drop Thy still dews of quietness,
Till all our strivings cease;

Take from our souls the strain and stress,
And let our ordered lives confess
The beauty of Thy peace.

—Whittier

I Think About God

I think about God,
     But I talk of small matters
Now isn't it odd
     How my idle tongue chatters
Of quarrelsome neighbors,
     Fine weather, and rain,
Indifferent labors,
     Indifferent pain,
Some trivial style
     Fashion shifts with a nod,
And yet, all the while,
     I am thinking of God.

—Gamaliel Bradford

Keep Silence, Friends

Keep silence, friends, for some have come
     To cast their care on God today;
And some to praise from thankful hearts;
     And some "Thy Kingdom come" to pray.
Keep silence; let Him speak anew
     To every heart—perhaps to you.

—E.B.R.

21. THANKSGIVING

PRAISE GOD THROUGH YOUR OCCUPATION

Ephesians 5:20—always and for everything giving thanks in the name of our Lord Jesus Christ to God the Father.

"How sharper than a serpent's tooth it is to have a thankless child." These words of Shakespeare apply all the more to God's children, to us. In every conceivable way we give affront to God. Our talents, our friends, our material wealth all draw their share of praise. But the One who gave us both our life and His is ignored. Do you have money? God is the giver. Do you have ability? Thank God for it.

The Apostle Paul would have us thanking God always. Surely he knew that men must work and concentrate on their vocations—surely Paul knew a person cannot remain on his knees every minute of the day. But Paul knew also that every person is a child of God. Therefore all our actions should be to God's glory. "What ever your task, work heartily, as serving the Lord and not men" (Colossians 3:23). Are you a farmer, merchant, housewife? Whatever your occupation, praise God through it.

Your lips need not move if your heart is in communion with Him.

—Conrad Crow

I Thank Thee, Lord

I thank thee, not for miracles perhaps,
    But for each simple, ordinary thing
That has no price—the gold of daffodils,
    The charm of peach trees in the early spring.

I would give thanks for mountains looming high,
    For crimson clover shining in the sun,
The scent of honeysuckle on the breeze,
    And peace of twilight when the day is done.

The carefree laughter of a child I love,
    The poignant sweetness of a rose in bloom,
My heart grows tender when I think of these,
    Of books and lamplight waiting in my room.

For work that keeps me happy and content,
    For memories of beauty I once knew,
I would give thanks for dreams of future joy,
    For friends whose words are always kind and true.

Oh, miracles deserve a song of praise,
    And eloquence like that I do not know,
But for the simple, ordinary things
    My heart with gratitude does overflow.

        By permission of Marjorie McMahan

Harvest

Thank God for harvest time of year
    For ripened grain that marks each row

Where sun and showers came to cheer
    The hearts with faith enough to sow,
For fruit bins full to overflowing
    From many a frost-molested path,
For many gardens all summer growing
    To provide for Autumn's aftermath.
        Look up, my heart, and surely see
        The glories of His majesty!

But there are those with calloused hands
    Who bore the brunt to heap our hoard;
Even now their empty storehouse stands—
    No horn of plenty there outpoured.
If "God from whom all blessings flow"
    Be praised on this Thanksgiving Day,
We must remember those who know
    Misfortune's cold, penurious way—
        Remember—then let voices ring
        With harvest praises to our King.

—Ruby Dell Baugher
From Crescent Hill Baptist Church Bulletin

22. TIME

Let every corner of this day
Become an altar, Lord for Thee.
A quiet place where I can pray
And hear Thee talk to me.

The bright expectancy of dawn
Will not endure the noon day heat

Unless refreshing strength is drawn
Where altars touch Thy feet.

—Sybil Leonard Armes

Time worketh, let me work too;
Time undoeth; let me do;
Busy as time my work I'll ply
Till I rest in the rest of eternity.

Sin worketh; let me work too;
Sin undoeth; let me do;
Busy as sin my work I'll ply
Till I rest in the rest of eternity.

O soul, this day is thine to imitate!
Be thou a day clothed in the living light!
Rise to thy task, and, be it small or great,
Shine on it till thy smile has made it bright;
Smile, smile on all thy duties, and beyond!
Thy life, like day, shall walk in robes of gold.

—Anonymous

The best things are nearest—breath in your nos-
trils, light in your eyes, flowers at your feet, duties at
your hand, the path of God just before you. Then do
not grasp at the stars, but do life's plain, common work
as it comes, certain that daily duties and daily bread
are the sweetest things of life.

—Anonymous

But this I call to mind,
    and so I have hope:
That the gracious deeds of the Lord never cease
    his compassion never fails;
They are fresh every morning;
    great is his faithfulness.

                  —Lamentations 3:21–23

O God, give me strength to live another day. Let me not turn coward before its difficulties or prove recreant to its duties. Let me not lose faith in my fellow man. Keep me sweet and sound of heart, in spite of ingratitude, treachery or meanness. Preserve me from minding little stings or giving them. Help me to keep my heart clean and to live honestly. Inspire me with the spirit of joy and gladness, and make me a cup of strength to suffering souls. Amen.

              —Adapted from Phillips Brooks

TIME

The man usually credited with founding modern socialism was the Count de Saint-Simon, a young French aristocrat who ordered his valet to wake him daily with the words, "Get up, monsieur le comte, remember, you have great things to do!"

              —Gerald Kennedy

"Lost; Somewhere between sunset and sunrise: two golden hours. Each set with sixty diamond minutes. No reward is offered because they are gone forever." Here is a little advertisement which ought to be written in letters of flame on our conscience.

—Patrick Mahony, in *You Can Find a Way*

Look well to this day!
For it is life; the very life of life.
In its brief course lie all the verities
    And realities of your existence.
The bliss of growth, the glory of action,
The splendor of beauty;
For yesterday is only a dream,
Tomorrow only a vision;
But today, well lived, makes of every yesterday
A dream of happiness and of every tomorrow
    A vision of hope.
Look well, therefore, to this day.

—Anonymous.

THE HAPPIEST HEART

Who drives the horses of the sun
    Shall lord it but a day;
Better the lowly deed were done,
    And kept the humble way.

The rust will find the sword of fame,
    The dust will hide the crown;
Aye, none shall nail so high his name
    Time will not tear it down.

The happiest heart will ever beat
 Was in some quiet breast
That found the common daylight sweet,
 And left to Heaven the rest.

    —John Vance Cheney

JUST FOR TODAY

Just for today, my Saviour—
 Tomorrow is not mine;
Just for today, I ask Thee,
 For light, and help divine;
Tomorrow's care I must not bear,
 The future is all Thine.

Today I bring my measure
 To Thee, that Thou might'st fill
And bless it, Lord, and teach me
 To trust and to be still.
Today I'd be, my God, for Thee,
 And do Thy holy will.

Just for today, my Saviour
 For ere the morrow break
Thy voice may call me unto Thee,
 And I shall no more walk
The desert path with need of faith,
 But face to face shall talk.

And if I have enough, Lord,
 Today, why should I grieve

Because of what I have not,
　　And may not need to have?
Each day, I pray Thee, have Thy way,
　　And I will trust Thy love.

　　　　　　　　　　—Helen McDowell

EACH NEW DAY A NEW BEGINNING

"New every morning is the love
Our wakening and uprising prove,
Through sleep and darkness safely brought
Restored to life, and power, and thought."

　　　　　　　　　　—John Keble

"To begin every day as if it were opening for the first time into the freshness and vibrancy of expectant living is to enter into the joy of the morning as a spiritual experience. We cannot sever ourselves from yesterday, but we need not add to yesterday's burden.

"One friend understood a little better, one prejudice rooted out, one slight forgiven, one measure of good will fortified each day—think what mighty opportunities lie hidden within the next circling of day and night."

　　　　　　　　　　—Max A. Kapp

23. YOUTH

Rejoice, O young man, in thy youth; and let thy heart cheer thee in the days of thy youth, and walk in the ways of thine heart, and in the sight of thine eyes;

but know thou, that for all these things God will bring thee into judgment.

—Ecclesiastes 11:9

Bestow thy youth so that thou mayest have comfort to remember it when it hath forsaken thee, and not to sigh and grieve at the account thereof. While thou art young thou wilt think it will never have an end; but the longest day hath its evening, and thou shalt enjoy it but once; it never turns again; use it therefore as the spring time, which soon departeth and wherein thou oughtest to plant and sow all provisions for a long and happy life.

—Sir Walter Raleigh.

If I had the opportunity to say a final word to all the young people of America, it would be this; Don't think too much about yourselves. Try to cultivate the habit of thinking of others; this will reward you. Nourish your minds by good reading; discover what your life work is, work in which you can be happiest. Be unafraid in all things where you know you are right. Be unselfish. That's the first and final commandment for those who would be useful and happy in their usefulness.

—Charles William Eliot

O soul, this day is thine to imitate!
Be thou a day clothed in the living light!
Rise to thy task, and, be it small or great,

Shine on it till thy smile has made it bright;
Smile, smile on all thy duties, and beyond!
Thy life, like day, shall walk in robes of gold.

—Anonymous.

ATTAINMENT

Use all your hidden forces. Do not miss
    The purpose of this life, and do not wait
For circumstances to mold or change your fate.
    In your own self lies destiny, Let this
Vast truth cast out all fear, all prejudice,
    All hesitation. Know that you are great,
Great with divinity. So dominate
    Environment, and enter into bliss—
Love largely and hate nothing. Hold no aim
    That does not chord with universal good.
Hear what the voices of the silence say,
    All joys are yours if you put forth your claim,
Once let the spiritual laws be understood,
    Material things must answer and obey.

—Ella Wheeler Wilcox

HOLD HIGH THE TORCH

Hold high the torch!
You did not light its glow—
'Twas given you by other hands, you know.
'Tis yours to keep it burning bright.
Yours to pass on when you need no more light;
For there are other feet that we must guide,

And other forms go marching by our side;
Their eyes are watching every smile and tear
And efforts which we think are not worth while,
Are sometimes just the very helps they need,
Actions to which their souls would give most heed;
So that in turn they hold it high
And say, "I watched someone else carry it this way."
If brighter paths should beckon you to choose,
Would your small gain compare with all you'd lose?

Hold high the torch!
You did not light its glow—
'Twas given you by other hands, you know.
I think it started down its pathway bright,
The day the Maker said: "Let there be light"
And He, once said, who hung on Calvary's tree—
"Ye are the light of the world"—Go!—Shine—for me.

—Anonymous

Prayer for Heroism

Dear God, please help my heart to know
That heroes do not always fight in armor
Or with sword to show
That they uphold the good and right.
The true hero can endure
Without resentment, and he knows
That victory is made more sure
By gentle words instead of blows.

The truest hero does not cease
In earnest efforts day by day;
He loves his God, his foes, and peace,
And scatters kindness on his way.
He lives to make a better world,
A chance to serve he does not miss;
His flag of honor is unfurled,
God, make me truly brave like this.

—John Martin

ACKNOWLEDGMENTS

The author wishes to express appreciation to the contributors of articles, and also to poets and publishers who very generously have granted permission to use extracts from their copyrighted publications. Appreciation is also extended to school, club and business periodicals for permission to reprint certain materials.

Among those to whom such acknowledgments are due are the following:

The Wayside Pulpit, 25 Beacon Street, Boston 8, Massachusetts, for "Bulletin Board Sentences."

Home Life Magazine, published by the Sunday School Board of the Southern Baptist Convention for "Blessings of Evening."

Strength, published by The Radio Gospel Fellowship for several articles and poems.

The Evangelical Publishers, Toronto, Canada, for poems by Annie Johnson Flint.

The Texas and Pacific Railway Company for three articles on "Faith."

Cosmopolitan Magazine for Irwin Edman's, "How to Begin a Month."

Red Book Magazine and Angelo Patri for the article entitled "You Don't Believe in Miracles," reprinted with their permission.

Mr. Howard Gillings for special permission to quote "Just for Today" by Helen McDowell.

W. B. Conkey and Company, a division of Rand McNally and Company, for permission to quote "Attainment" by Ella Wheeler Wilcox.

Thomas C. Clark for permission to quote "New Year" and "A Prayer for Teachers," from *One Thousand Quotable Poems,* Harper & Brothers, New York, N. Y.

Yale University Press for permission to quote "I Think About God" from *Shadow Verses* by Gamaliel Bradford.

Your Life Magazine for permission to quote "A Quiet Place" by Elsie Robinson. (This feature copyrighted by the Kingsway Press, Inc.)

Special appreciation is given to Miss Frances Floyd, Alumnus Secretary, Mercer University, Macon, Ga., for initial research work in the compilation of material for *BETTER CHURCH BULLETINS.*

An earnest effort has been made to locate the authors of all copyrighted selections. However, in some instances addresses could not be found. If there is any oversight, the author will make proper acknowledgment in future editions of this book.